Barack Obama

by Grace Hansen

ABDO
UNITED STATES
PRESIDENT BIOGRAPHIES
Kids

www.abdopublishing.com

Published by Abdo Kids, a division of ABDO, PO Box 398166, Minneapolis, Minnesota 55439.

Copyright © 2015 by Abdo Consulting Group, Inc. International copyrights reserved in all countries.
No part of this book may be reproduced in any form without written permission from the publisher.

Printed in the United States of America, North Mankato, Minnesota.

052014

092014

 THIS BOOK CONTAINS
RECYCLED MATERIALS

Photo Credits: AP Images, Shutterstock, Thinkstock, The White House, © Pete Souza / FEMA
© ChameleonsEye p.15, © Solphoto p.17, © spirit of america p.19 / Shutterstock

Production Contributors: Teddy Borth, Jennie Forsberg, Grace Hansen

Design Contributors: Candice Keimig, Laura Rask, Dorothy Toth

Library of Congress Control Number: 2013953024

Cataloging-in-Publication Data

Hansen, Grace.

 Barack Obama / Grace Hansen.

   p. cm. -- (United States president biographies)

ISBN 978-1-62970-086-1 (lib. bdg.)

Includes bibliographical references and index.

1. Obama, Barack--Juvenile literature. 2. Presidents--United States--Biography--Juvenile literature.
3. Racially mixed people--United States--Biography--Juvenile literature. I. Title.

973.932--dc23

[B]   2013953024

Table of Contents

Early Life

Barack Obama was born
on August 4, 1961. He was
born in Hawaii.

Hawaii

5

Obama's parents **divorced** when he was a child. His grandparents helped raise him.

Obama was a good student. He

went to college and law school.

9

Obama spent time with the

Chicago, Illinois community.

He helped people unite

to make a difference.

Family

Obama has a wife named Michelle. They have two daughters. Their names are Sasha and Malia.

12

Becoming President

Obama became a **state senator**.

He later became a **US senator**.

In 2008, Obama was **elected** the 44th US president.

Presidency

Obama is the first African American president in US history. He was **elected** president two times.

Many people believe in
Obama. He works hard
to help people in need.

More Facts

- Obama's favorite sport is basketball.

- Obama went by the name Barry when he was a child.

- Obama's father and mother **divorced** when he was young. He rarely saw his father, who lived in Kenya, Africa.

Glossary

divorce – when a marriage between two people legally ends.

elected – to be chosen by a voting system.

state senator – a member elected by districts within their home states. They represent their districts when voting.

US senator – a member of the US Senate. The US Senate makes up a part of Congress. Two senators are elected from each state. The two senators represent their home state in Washington, D.C.

23

Index

abdokids.com

Use this code to log on to abdokids.com and access crafts, games, videos and more!

Abdo Kids Code:
UBK0861